I0489953

This Book is designed as a primer and overview of internet marketing and online business for beginners.

As a cruiser or wannabe cruiser, one of the most difficult obstacles to overcome is making a living while sailing and enjoying the cruising lifestyle.
The Internet can really level the playing field and allow anyone to make a decent living without having to work a 9-5 job.

In this book you will discover an overview of all of the avenues of internet marketing available to you. Once you have a basic understanding of what's available you can begin to narrow things down to what kind of internet business will fit best with your skills, interests and overall goals.

One of the biggest problems facing people new to internet business and online marketing is overwhelm. Please don't let the amount of information out there overwhelm you. It can be broken down in to simple easy to master steps.

My website Http://moneyforcruising.com is a great place to start. I created this site to help other cruisers chart their course to the cruising lifestyle.

What is Internet Marketing?

Internet marketing is really one of the most versatile and lucrative business opportunities that is possible today.

It deals with the marketing of products and or services over the internet to a specific demographic or throughout the world. Basically, you will be leveraging on the power of the internet and its spread to find prospective consumers and make them customers.

The main purpose of internet marketing is to take advantage of the internet as a medium to sell products and services which will satisfy a broader range of consumers than are available in a single location.

Internet marketing is also a very valuable method of providing information to these consumers in a way that will help convince them to make a purchase.

The way this works is simple, as many of the products and services available online are at about the same price of those available in stores, the internet makes them easily available and a very convenient location to shop. The internet also allows for products and services which are not available nearby to be purchased and used by customers.

This makes it possible for anyone to sell nearly anything regardless of their geographic location. Internet marketing opens up several opportunities for you to create revenue streams by becoming a marketer online.

You can either sell your own products and services or go about selling products and services created by someone else. To accomplish this, you will need to apply strategies and techniques which will use the internet in a way that will help you reach and exceed your marketing goals. We will learn this later on in this course.

But first, let's take a look at the most common types of websites that people use to make money online with...

Understanding Blogs

The term blog refers to a shared online journal website. It is a mash-up of the words web and log to create blog.

Blogs are a way to provide commentary about opinions as well as various forms of information which can be provided via blogging. Blogging rapidly became popular in the late 90s around the turn of the millennium and has continued to grow.

Blogging itself has evolved as an option which can be used to market online to followers of the blog. Blog followers tend to be readers who are interested in what the blogger has to write about nearly every subject. The possibility of getting a reader to be interested in a blog is very high depending on which niche the blog deals with.

The blog can reflect on a certain niche with a great deal of information into the subject matter and attract more followers over time. Blogs have been observed to maintain steady growth of followers which could then be marketed to later on.

A blog that continues to grow is simple to maintain by having the writer provide a posting or blurb on a related subject. These tidbits of information will spark the interest of blog followers and keep the blog populated with regular readers.

Once the blog owner has enough followers, they can really market to their readers by plugging products or providing advertising on their blogs.

Either way, they can make money based on their influence and the popularity of the blogs that are being updated. A fairly populated blog can really rake in large amounts of revenue from their readers that are interested in what is marketed through the blog interface.

Examples of Blog Uses:

Daily Journal

This is often the most common use of a blog by the traditional user that just wants to keep a blog. They will use the blog to write about what happened in the day, any thoughts or ideas that they had and enjoy sharing with others who are interested in reading. These are more to the effect of a personal diary with the element of publicity.

Corporate Blogging

These are a blog type which is used for business interests. These can be used to help create a brand, develop marketing as well as being an option that is useful for public relations. These corporate blogs are very useful for boosting the image of the business or corporation. These are also more than likely possible to be group managed which allows several moderators have the ability to post content to the blog under a variety of aliases.

These are the ultimate tool for providing information about what the business does to help out the community, lower industrial costs and much more. This will help the business get on the good side of their customers.

Niche Blogs

These are also fairly common and are designed to offer information on a subject of interest. These types of the blogs are the ones which are targeted the most by internet marketers. They can focus on just about any field such as politics, travel, housing, fashion, education, art, music, etc. The reason why they work so well for internet marketing is the fact that they are so focused.

This makes it easier to advertise to the interests of the audience based on their tastes. If you are able to hit upon their tastes, you advertising and internet marketing will work much better on them.

Media Blogs

The media blogs are a newer type of blog which works much better with the faster internet connections and the demand for entertainment that requires less thinking power. These are very simple to maintain and only require that the blogger offers content for their followers to enjoy.

The content can be anything from artwork, photography, music, videos and even interactive games. Media blogs can reuse content in several ways which makes them the simplest to keep populated. Media content can just as easily be spun and reticulated into new content to be offered to followers to enjoy.

Blogs are naturally one of the attention-grabbing forms of online entertainment that are available today. Several blog services are designed specifically to provide an outlet to sell to the audience while others are designed to be used strictly as a journal. Utilizing the former is what internet marketing will aim to work towards.

Internet Marketing Websites

Websites are another form of marketing which can really be turned into a powerhouse for selling anything and everything that the consumer wishes to purchase. These websites can generate a large amount of traffic to the pages or simply reroute the traffic to another location where the sale can be made. Websites can employ a very diverse range of tactics which make it possible for traffic to be generated to the site.

The reason why a large amount of traffic is good is simply because the more visitors to the site there are, the higher the possibility is that those visitors will decide to make a purchase of an item that is made available via the site.

Internet marketing plays on a simple fact that there is always a buyer for products or services and the job of the marketing is to make its way to the customer using whatever means necessary to get the sale. There are four main business models which make up the majority of internet marketing websites and they are:

E-commerce Sites

This model of internet marketing is designed to make it possible for the business to sell directly to the consumer. The main concept for internet marketing through e-commerce sites is to create a virtual store where the consumers can visit and shop much like they would at any other physical store.

This convenience makes it possible for a wide variety of prices to be charged for products based on availability and the demand of the market for the products or services.

Lead Sites

Creating traffic to a website based on value of the information can be a very easy way to generate sales leads. This is the purpose of lead sites which can generate traffic which will more than likely be interested in the products or services that are offered by the business.

These lead sites work based on the value of the content and what the website creator can offer to the user in terms of information, tools or other forms of usability. Sales will generally be completed based on the need to further inquire more about something or fulfilling a necessary function that was not available for free.

Affiliate Marketing

Affiliate marketing through websites and other means is the process of selling products or services that are created by an entity and sharing in the profits from the sale. Affiliate marketing makes it possible for beginners to jump into the marketing service and start receiving revenue by marketing an already complete project.

This cuts out the need to develop a product or service which could take a great deal of time and money to invest into the process of marketing. This is one of the most common methods of getting into internet marketing which provides a simpler inlet into the system of selling products and services to others.

Local Marketing Sites

The process of local marketing is one of the options that can be done with a website. Using the internet to provide options for real world and local applications can be accomplished in several ways.

This option really makes it possible to start online sales to local businesses and locations. This can be accelerated using social platforms online which can help to route local traffic to the websites which are offering local trade and business. Local marketing can actually reduce the costs of shipping by making it possible to deliver without using an external service to move product to its final destination.

Websites can be used as an extension of the business or company to provide its products or services to its consumers. Websites are a versatile internet marketing tool which should not be overlooked and taken advantage of whenever possible.

Websites are also one of the most convincing marketing materials for marketing because they take time to create and are more credible than a simple conversation with a salesperson.

Since websites are more than likely to be made interactive in some way, they can garner much more attention by their audience. A well composed website can keep a visitor on the site exploring into the information and helping them learn more about the products and services.

The more information that the visitors are receiving with their time on the site, the better educated they become about the products. If they feel that they know more than enough about the products, they can mentally weight them and their usefulness in their lives which may lead to a purchasing decision.

The website can also help to promote this need to make a purchase of an item. Persuasion to make a purchase can play on many psychological levels or simply made possible by providing the right environment for the visitor to feel comfortable enough to make a purchase. The atmosphere of the website also plays a key role in generating sales.

Areas of Internet Marketing

Internet marketing will take various forms which are all accessible by anyone willing to take the time and put in the effort to achieve a successful internet marketing campaign.

By understanding and applying the areas of internet marketing into your campaign, you will be able to generate sales and create lasting streams of revenue which will last for some time with minimal upkeep.

Each and every area of internet marketing that you can explore will offer more opportunities to reach more people and have greater opportunities to turn potential consumers into repeat customers.

The better you are at marketing the products, the further your marketing methods will reach and your customers may actually come in from all around the world to purchase whatever it is that you are selling.

Affiliate Marketing on the Internet

One of areas of the internet marketing practices is affiliate marketing. This process is really a referral program that is designed to reward a seller for corralling customers and getting them to purchase a product or service.

This reward can be a generous percentage of the total cost of each item sold and can easily make the affiliate marketer some money based on their sales figures.

Affiliate marketing is very versatile because it can be done nearly anywhere. Many of the methods include marketing the product in organic search engine results, through advertisements, email marketing and even display marketing such as television commercials. This can greatly increase the exposure of the affiliate marketing to a greater audience which could lead to more sales.

The most common form of affiliate marketing is driving traffic to the product seller's website in an attempt to generate a sale. The websites that the traffic is directed to will usually have a large amount of marketing and sales copy available in an effort to convert the visitors into customers which in turn equals revenue for both the affiliate and the product creator/seller.

This is often one of the preferred methods for product designers to make money off of their products. They themselves simply need to get others interested in selling their products or services for them and provide compensation based on performance.

If no sales are made by a marketer, then no money is given to that marketer. The more sales that are completed, the more money is generated for the product creator and the internet marketer will receive a great compensation for their work generating the sales.

In this way the product creator will only have to pay for the sales that have been made while still receiving a cut while doing close to nothing.

Implementation of affiliate marketing is very simple and may be done using an existing program or can be done through experimentation with several different options in selling through internet marketing.

The product creator will either be using their own software to provide affiliate marketing or they will be using a third party service which can simplify the process and make it possible for anyone to try their hand at affiliate marketing.

A large number of coaxing methods are used to get visitors to affiliate landing pages to make a purchase. Observing everything from offering a limited time deal to making it possible to click something on the page to reveal a discount code which will provide the product or service at a fraction of the cost is employed to generate the sales of the product or service.

While this may be effective, this makes the total sales cost go down and will generate less money for both the affiliate and the product creator.

Selling Your Own Products on the Internet

Internet marketing to sell your own products is possible in several ways. One of the main things to look into and understand is whether or not you will be offering physical products when you sell.

Physical products can and will make money when marketed correctly but they will often have some disadvantages:

Stock

You will need to always have some of the product on hand to sell it to others. If you do not have the product available then you will not be able to sell it. This means that you will also need to have the materials to produce the products or have some means to create more once they have depleted their available stock and there is more interest.

Storage

Having stock on hand is one thing but storing overstock is never easy. Unless the product creator has a warehouse to store large amounts of stock that isn't being used right away, they will have to store it elsewhere which may impede on their personal space.

Shipping

The product creator would then need to be able to process orders and ship them out to their appropriate customers who have made purchases of their product. Having multiple products only complicates this matter worse.

Overstock

Being overstocked makes this process even worse with physical goods to sell. Not being able to sell a portion of the stock will force the product
creator to stay with an order of unsold product which may be an extra expense down the line.

Internet marketing with no physical products can reduce these problems greatly. An internet product or service which can be delivered electronically will not require the seller to have it in stock, take up an insane amount of storage, have to incur shipping costs and does not need to be pitted into a problem where overstock causes a loss of funds.

In fact, common options for internet marketing will tent to choose electronic products such as books, audio books and other products which will are automatically dispensed to buyers once payment is made.

CPA Marketing on the Internet

CPA or Cost Per Action, is an online advertising option for internet marketing which is very useful for those who can convince others to perform and complete criteria which in turn will pay the marketer upon completion. An advertiser will usually have several different actions which they will pay out to their marketers for completing each of the actions. Some of these CPA options include:

Purchases

Whenever a customer completes a purchase of a product or service, the marketer that is credited will receive proper compensation for their sale. These are very similar to affiliate marketing options where the marketer gets paid a portion for each sale that they make via a commission.

Submissions

For completing a form, filling out a survey or managing to enter information of some sort, internet marketers can generate a large amount of data for market research or other needs. They will need to get the potential consumers to fill out the forms though.

The selection of different submission options will tend to also make it a versatile option to allow for actions to complete and earn money through.

Downloads

Having a visitor download a file which then reports to the business via either a download link or a reporting feature of the downloaded file. This then credits the marketer for routing visitors to the download link and has been accessed by visitors. This option may be very slow moving and may pay out after long periods of time.

Installations

This is one of the most valuable options for CPA partners to try and get their audience to do. The payment terms are through a download and installation of software to their computer system. Many of these installation distributions will have marketing in mind and will track the installer to gain more information about their habits.

This provides vital information to the developers to help them create better products to release later on. Many of these installations are filtered out by antivirus and spyware removal software because of these data collection tendencies and will remove them before they are credited to a CPA account.

Advertisers consider this type of marketing the optimal advertising option because they can control exactly what to pay their marketers for and only if they complete the requirements each time.

Another form of this is known as CPL or Cost Per Lead, which pays for qualifying leads which may or may not lead to a direct sale. These are generally less strict but still require vital steps to be completed by visitors before any grant is offered to the marketer.

Promoting Offline Business Online

Internet marketing does not simply pertain to marketing online. One of the surprising uses of internet marketing is promotion. Promoting an offline business online does two important functions.

First off, the offline businesses get an online presence, which means that they can be located online and will show up in search results. The second function is increasing the reach of the business to a greater audience. This exposure is a very good thing which can help to introduce new customers to a business and improve the overall business dealings of the company.

Promotion of businesses online really helps to get the word out about what that business does. It helps to communicate the idea of what the business can do for you, what problems they can fix and how you can reach them. It is a perfect opportunity to get the information for a service that you may really be in need of at the time.

An online presence provides a way to let everyone know that a business really exists. This is very useful, especially towards legitimizing the business and letting everyone know about it and where it can be found, who owns it and much more pieces of information which may not be transmitted over other mediums.

Emails are also another common method of promotion for an offline business. Those who have a way to market out to emails in a local area can really spread and promote a local business quickly and efficiently.

The one drawback to emails is the fact that you have to be authorized to send emails to someone otherwise it is spam and can have some real legal implications. Using an email list can help to market out to interested parties via email.

Unit Two : Internet Marketing Skills

You will need to develop your internet marketing skills before venturing out with any internet marketing plan or scheme. If not you may end up spending money where it is not needed and losing more than you are actually making.

This is not productive use of your time and efforts. So it is important to learn what each of these skills is used for and why they are useful to your marketing future.

Composing an arsenal of these valuable skills is one of the most important things that you could do in your internet marketing preparation.

Knowing more about these skills will definitely provide you with several options to try whenever you are performing your internet marketing tasks.

Niche Research: Uncovering "Markets"

Niche research is the time you put into learning what your market is in terms of profitability and strength.

The more you know about your niche the better and that is proven by the results that you will see with each niche you experiment with.

Going into a field where you hardly know anything about the niche is really a bad move for two very good reasons.

First, you are entering a marketing domain where many others are experts on the subject. Second, you will struggle to work well in the environment for the niche because you know little to nothing about the niche.

Now if you think you do not know anything about any niches in the first place, you are wrong. Think about something that interests you personally to a greater extent than most other topics.

This is a good niche to research into. The reason why it is a better niche is simple as you will already have some knowledge about the niche and you will know where to find more information about the niche market you are interested in.

Knowing that the niche has a passionate audience in place is always a great start. When you know that others are interested in the niche because of the niche itself, you can ensure that the niche will be getting a large amount of traffic.

If a niche is really boring then there may not really be an audience to market to. This would be very disastrous for your internet marketing because you will not have many people to market to.

Being interested in a niche is already a step forward in the right direction. This ensures that you are able to focus on the niche and understand more about the topics that are discussed.

You can learn more about the scope of the niche such as the general niche that stems all of the sub-niches. This is useful in determining whether or not you will be centered on marketing to a broader audience or to a specialized audience instead. To understand what we are discussing we will look at an example niche:

Broad Niche

Crafts can be a very broad niche. It can encompass a large variety of crafts that can include everything from simple artwork creation using craft materials to highly specialized artistry which could retail for hundreds of thousands of dollars.

General Niche

Jewelry is a sub niche of crafts. Although it is still very general in terms of what the niche is describing, it is more specific than just crafts. Jewelry can be art or fashion and can range in price from cheap to expensive.

Jewelry also gives a basic idea of what you will be dealing with once you narrow down the options for the niche.

Narrow Niche

Rings are a sub niche of jewelry and can still be quite broad. There are several types of rings which are possible to focus on. A narrow niche is always a great option to try to market because you will be less likely to run out of ideas for marketing.

The ring niche is still not as narrow as you can go for a niche but it is somewhat close.

Specialized Niche

Gold Engagement Ring is a specialized niche. You are getting down to the very products that are going to be of interest to the traffic (potential customers) that you will be marketing to.

The engagement ring niche is commonly held towards the gold metal because of tradition even through there are so many options for gold engagement rings. You could still make the niche more specific still though...

Specific or Extremely Targeted Niche

People interested in Tiffany & Co. Gold Engagement Rings is a very specific niche and your traffic for the niche will be directly from these keywords when they are trying to find your online marketing materials. These specific niches can be easy to work with or difficult to work with depending on the niche and how much competition there is for the niche.

If you want to check the competition for your niche, you have two main options:

The first option is to search your niche on a search engine. It is recommended that you try a basic search at http://www.google.com .

For example, we will use the niche keywords that we used in the previous examples:

"Crafts" receives roughly 269,000,000 results (rounded)
"Jewelry" receives roughly 526,000,000 results (rounded)
"Rings" receives roughly 238,000,000 results (rounded)
"Gold Engagement Ring" receives roughly 5,700,000 results (rounded)
"Tiffany & Co. Gold Engagement Ring" receives roughly 558,000 results (rounded)

We could keep getting more specific with our searches as well. Each time you get more specific, there will generally be fewer results.

There are some keywords that do get a lot of attention for some reason so this will not be true all of the time.

To show how narrow the results get with one more level, we will search for "Tiffany & Co. 18K Yellow Gold Tiffany

Engagement Ring Setting" which yields only 55,000 results (rounded).

As you can see, the more specific you get with your search, the fewer results there are. This will help you to gauge the market density for your niche.

Of course, you will not want to get so specific with your search terms as most people will not type out that much when running a search on Google.

The second option is to look into the Google Trends: http://www.google.com/trends

With Google trends you can type in your niche and see how often it is searched for. This way you can understand how often your internet marketing efforts may actually be seen by your potential audience once everything is in place.

You can also use the Google Trends service to compare multiple niche keywords with each other to choose a more viable one from the list.

Remember that you do not need to stick directly to one niche, you could market to multiple sub niches within a broader one just as easily with more chances at greater results in the future.

Even with a good amount of traffic, you still need to determine whether or not the niche can be monetized. We can understand that jewelry is a profitable niche for the artisans that create the jewelry. To an internet marketer, profit comes in many forms.

Monetization is the ability to turn something into a stream of revenue.

Even with a good niche keyword with a low amount of competition such as "Tiffany's Engagement Ring", an estimated amount that you would receive from Google AdWords would be $2 per click. The estimated amount of daily clicks would be less than one per day for that keyword so you would be lucky to get a few in per month with some aggressive marketing.

It is a great idea to check all of these parameters with the Google AdWords Keyword tool available at:

http://www.adwords.google.com/select/keywordtoolexternal

SEO and Traffic Generation

One of the major skills that you need to lean is SEO (Search Engine Optimization) and Traffic Generation. What SEO sums up to is creating content and optimizing said content so that it is properly indexed by search engine spiders.

Spiders, also known as web crawlers, robots, bots and other technical names are special programs which are designed to go out and find new content that has not been indexed into the databases and directory of Google (as well as other search engines).

SEO can be done in many different ways which can all contribute to the efficacy of the process.

The main thing that SEO is doing is taking advantage of how search engines and people work when they are searching for their keywords. Also taken into account is the search phrases that are used naturally by the audience and which search engines they use the most to access the search results from.

This is accomplished by a few sets of rules which have been determined to help influence how search results are displayed on the search engines:

Keywords

The one thing that helps search engines know what your traffic sources are looking for are keywords. Keywords help to route the search engine by telling it what should be relevant in the content that it is pulling from the index to show to you.

The content must contain the keywords you use unless the keywords are basically not used in any manner together, then suggested best matches are chosen for the results. Using a wide range of keywords for each piece of content is always a great way to make the content generate a lot of interest by Google. Only using 1-3 keywords per article is always recommended.

Keyword Density

The keyword density is the amount of times that the keyword appears in a piece of content on a website. It can be an article, some commentary or even within a page in the depths of the website. The keyword will show up any given number of times and that is the number that should be divided by the total number of words in the content.

This figure should then be multiplied by 100. The resulting number is the percentage of times the keyword was used within the document.

This percentage is the keyword density.

Density should stay within 3-15% of the total word count for the piece of content. Any more or using too many keywords can be considered keyword stuffing and that is not approved by Google.

Meta Tags

The meta tags are tags that tell the page what to display. They are data elements that show extra information to the browser about the content and who the author was, publication date, expiration date, the description of the page and much more.

This is the best way to make on page optimization for the content. Once complete, the search engines will have even more information to use when categorizing the results during an organic search by a user.

Backlinks

The backlinks are any links that come back to a page on your website or to any site where some content resides. Backlinks are very important towards telling Google which websites are more credible.

Basically, the more valid backlinks that are created, the more Google will think the website that those links are coming to are important. The stronger these links are coming from well established websites the better they help weigh towards the judgment for the website or content.

This will result in much better search result rankings for the pages that receive the best backlink sources.

Website Coding

The coding of your website is also one of the things that Google will take a look at. Having very low quality coding or many errors in the code such as excess and unnecessary code will count against the website.

It is a great idea to take the time to clean up the HTML or other coding used on the site in order to appeal to Google. It is best to keep all of the code as clean as possible while reducing the amount of errors that occur on the site coding in the future as well. This plays a role in how your website is ranked when compared to other websites that are either clean or messy as well.

There are two main types of SEO.

White Hat SEO

This is a term for a number of techniques which are used to create positive and long lasting effects for the optimization. These are known to not break the terms of service or website rules of Google and other search engines.

Black Hat SEO

These are SEO techniques designed to make a rapid improvement in the search engine rankings within a very short time span. These techniques are more likely to get the pages indexed and ranked higher more quickly but also make it possible for the website to be removed from Google for circumventing the natural ranking process.

Sites that are caught performing Black Hat SEO will normally remain delisted and unable to be relisted for a period of time or indefinitely.

Traffic Generation can also be done in lots of ways. The main thing about traffic generation is that all of the SEO preparations that are made will help to increase traffic over time. Increasing traffic via other methods is encouraged whenever possible. Leaving backlinks in various locations is sure to spark an interest in the site, especially if it is in locations where like minded people congregate.

One of the best things to try is to choose a web forum or group that deals with the same niche and post links to the site around in various locations. Each time this is done, you raise the chances of the website being visited via link traffic.

Understanding How Advertising Works

Copywriting

Copywriting a powerful and profitable skill to learn. Basically, the copy is the content that you are placing on your website or in various other locations that is being used to sell a product – the writing that SELLS>

There are several ways to get your copy to peak the interests of your readers.

These are 6 options to remember about copy which will more than likely speak to the readers on a level of interest which will make them pay attention and read each word to the end:

1. **Fears** -If you know what your audience fears, then you can understand how to manipulate them into listening. By knowing the problems of the audience, you can word your copy in a way that sounds like you will be able to solve their problems. This is a great way that you can gain their attention and keep their attention past the first few seconds.

2. **Language** - Keep in line with the mode of speech that your audience uses. If they are commonly on the verge of saying radical things then you should sound like that as well. You want them to feel like you are one of them and this is not an easy task. Of course your copy is going to be seen by dozens of people, hopefully hundreds and thousands later on. Make sure that you are on their level and understand what they want to hear from you. The more your efforts are to sound like your audience the easier it will be to hold their attention when you are talking about selling them something.

3. **Conversational Tone** - You want to sound like you are talking with your audience and not at them, the floor or anything else. A simple conversational tone is all it takes to help you connect just a little more when you are able to have a conversation with the audience even if they are only listening to what you have to say.

When you ask someone a question, you won't be able to really respond to their answer but instead you will be able to answer with them to help steer them in the direction you want them to be thinking in. This is very helpful towards selling pricier items because it helps the reader believe that what they will be doing is purchasing something that is within their acceptable budget range.

4. **Relationship** - In any exchange of message between you and your customers, you will want them to understand that you are there for them. They will want to believe that you are their friend and that you would never lie to them. Although this is partly true, you still want them to buy your products or whichever types of products that you are marketing. As long as you have your audience feeling like you is their friend they will be more responsive to your suggestions once you tell them to try all of the products, their free trials and other options that are available with them.

5. **Value** - Every time you are having an exchange with your customers you need them to know that what you are offering them is worth whatever the price they will end up paying in the end. The best way to do this is to itemize the total cost of each feature and say what the value is of whatever it is you are selling. Then you hook them with the low price that they will be paying to receive the larger value. This is the same technique that

telemarketers and infomercials use to hook the interest of impulse buyers.

6. **Sale** -No matter what, you need to tell your audience that you are trying to sell them something. This will let them know that they can buy it relatively soon and that they should take advantage of it right away.

Incorporate a sense of urgency for them to make the purchase whenever appropriate that way they will feel like they will need to make the purchase. Selling them on this sense of urgency is always a great way to get sales because the audience will believe that the window of opportunity is closing on them and they will have to make their purchase soon or else they will miss out on what is available for them at this price.

Conversions

These are the sales that are made after your audience reads your marketing materials such as your copy. The conversion rate is the percentage of conversions you receive from the total number of views of said marketing material.

You will want your conversions to be as high as possible, especially with your sales copy. The best method to accomplish this is to take advantage of writing a great copy page to start getting sales. If you need to, hiring a professional writer to create the copy may increase the number of conversions by improving how the copy reaches the audience.

AB Split Testing Your Advertising

AB split testing is generally a marketing practice that is designed to understand which elements of a marketing tactic are working best. This can be done with testing for a variety of different elements such as headers, formatting and tone of voice in the content.

The AB split testing is best used to better understand how visitor's behaviors are and what their priorities are once they are on your site and able to have a chance to look at what is available is always a great tool to understand how to change your marketing tactics.

AB split testing is also a great opportunity to solve problems with website pages or content that are not appearing correctly or are simply not rendered correctly. This can help you to troubleshoot your website and determine problems which may be hindering your conversions.

AB split testing is also a great method to use to try out something completely different to see what changes with your marketing tactics whenever you are trying to sell something. You could learn new designs for your content which are able to produce much more conversions for your site. You can test out small changes to complete pages or websites to see which are more responsive to get the best results out of the design of your site.

It is important to use AB split testing for a period of time to see what works best. The more tests you run with the AB split test, the greater the results will be and the diverse range of values can help you determine what is best for your pages so that you can make the most out of your advertising efforts using copy and other forms of sales generating materials.

Squeeze Pages

The squeeze page is a landing page that is specifically designed to offer a large amount of information for a direct marketing campaign. The squeeze page really helps the potential customers drop their guard when they reach a direct marketing website.

They will often state the privacy standards and policy that they will not share the email address with anyone and will outline exactly what the customer will be receiving if they decided to actually purchase the product.

The basic composition of a squeeze page is simple, it is a single web page that is designed to catch the email address of the visitor. The page will have absolutely no exit hyperlinks which could distract the visitor and make them leave the page. Instead, the page is highly optimized for search engine optimization to help ensure that it will show up in searches for the product that is being offered.

Key components of a squeeze page:

Testimonials

Testimonials are littered throughout the squeeze page that explains how well the product works. They will often be about success and how little time it took to reach that success. It makes it easier to get people to lower their guard about the product because after all, so many people are having such great success with it. There is no mention of how many people have not made any progress after making a purchase of the product.

Catchy Sales Copy

One of the great things about a squeeze page is the amount of work that is put into the copy. By wording the copy very nicely, readers are able to follow along well and keep their guard down once it has been lowered by a testimonial.

The copy will help to make connections with the reader which helps to make it seem like the writer was their friend. With this relationship created, the writer can pretty much tell the reader anything they like and they will more than likely believe it.

Bullets

Bullets denote key important portions of the squeeze page. Instead the bullets are able to trick you into seeing what the squeeze page creator wanted you to see.

These will often be used to tell you what you will be missing out on if you do not choose to use the product. Many of the reasons that are given are generic but make more personal and relayed to the reader in a more interpersonal tone which makes them feel like their friend is saying that they would be doing worse without it.

Teasers

These are short snippets of information that you will be able to peek inside of the product. The reader will be tempted to learn much more about the product once they have seen what is available in small portions.

This is a great psychological trick that helps the reader to become somewhat addicted to what they are reading. Giving a taste of something then saying that the rest is only available for the paid owners of the product really makes some people anxious and want to read more as soon as possible so they will try the product.

Bonuses

The bonuses are designed to tell the readers what they will be getting in addition to the plan that they are agreeing on for the product they are about to purchase. These bonuses are very simple to understand and will usually be tempting bonuses that are only available if you join before the deadline for the deal is over.

Bonuses such as extra products, free training and a variety of other offers are always favorites which can trick readers into believing that they would
be fools not to purchase the product because they would be missing out on all of the great products that are available with the complete package.

Deadlines

A deadline for the sale is almost always present with modern day squeeze pages. These are usually controlled via on page code that display the current day, time or other chronological configurations and it will give up to 24 hours to order the deal until it is over.

Even if you left the page open until the deadline passed and refreshed the page, the deadline would simply reset with the new time period. This simple trick will often cause those who are new to these types of pages to believe that they have a limited time to get the deal of their lifetime.

Scarcity

The scarcity rule uses the deadline rule to an extreme. It provides a coded clock that allows readers to see the clock ticking down for a countdown.

This clock will usually have a time limit – for example 60 seconds left before the deal is gone. This causes the reader to panic and in many events causing them to pay for the deal before the may fully understand it.

Again, these are simply coded in and it wouldn't matter if the reader was within the time frame or several days late, they will still be paying the same price and will receive all of the bonuses of they enter their email address.

Videos

Newer squeeze pages are incorporating videos. These videos are designed to show testimonials and other selling points about the product. It can even be a small infomercial that pressures the viewer into wanting to buy the product or else their life will not be as simple as they state is possible only with their product. Videos are very simple to implement thus they are becoming more common and effective as well.

Audio

Those which cannot deal with the videos on the squeeze page often use audio. Audio is very similar to the videos by providing auditory stimuli in one of many manners to help sell the product.

It could be the CEO of the company expressing their excitement that a new member is just a click away or some earnings figures that others have made with the system.

These are usually gimmicks that are very pleasant to hear by those who do not believe what they are reading. This is usually effective when coupled with several graphics that display earnings statements and graphs.

Guarantee

A guarantee is not included on all squeeze pages but they are common enough to be mentioned. Sometimes a marketer will want to guarantee that their product works well enough that they will risk giving you back your money if you ask for a refund within a period of time.

Usually these periods are unusually long with the purpose of keeping the person from thinking about a refund so that they simply just forget about it and the guarantee rolls over, nullifying.

The only clickable links that are actually available on the page are those to submit information to the service. The information that they are mining for is the email address so that they can offer more information about the product as well as related products that will more than likely interest the reader.

Now that Google and other search engines are requiring more content on the squeeze pages to be able to rank, it is not impossible for you to come across an embellished squeeze page from time to time. These are pages that come with a variety of information available on them which help them rank without looking like a spam website through Google's updated search algorithms.

Thank You Pages

A thank you page is where the customer is sent after they either provide their email address or have made a purchase of a product. This is an important page because it can be used in a few ways. Each option will usually help improve the relationship with the customer. This makes it possible to squeeze even more out of them if you can manage that.

Most thank you pages are very plain and will usually only offer a small glimpse of a thank you text with a return link. This is a very inefficient use of the thank you page. A thank you page should be optimized in a way to be colorful but not disturbing to the eyes. The page should also incorporate more than just the words "Thank You" after they have agreed to provide a sale or their information.

The first thing that you could do is customize the page to fit the rest of the website. This can be a simple template change to make the page match. The reason why this is recommended is simple, as no one wants to be greeted with an unsavory and unexciting page that simply states thank you. It may make them feel as you have simply taken their money then booted them off of the website. Once this is completed you can update what the page has to say.

The simplest thing to do is make the text more personal. You can say thank you for being a customer and boast that only smart and reliable customers get to the thank you page. Another message that makes a great impression is always a good idea to look into. Any number of other messages can be used to help make the thank you page a little bit more personable and friendly to land on once a purchase has been completed.

Last, you can place advertisements around the thank you page to help promote other products. This way you could possibly get a double commission from two separate products.

When you allow your customers to make their way to the thank you page, it is tailored to help them find other amazing deals which they may not be able to live without. You can even make the page simple and ask your preferred customers to continue shopping with your service. Simply asking a small request like this will usually set the action into motion.

Social Sharing

This is also a great idea that is very simple to implement using modern tools available directly from the social media services such as http://www.Facebook.com and http://www.Twitter.com .

These social buttons can help your customers refer new customers from their very own friends.

Let me tell you why this is a very amazing prospect… people are more than likely going to trust their friend's recommendation on a social networking platform when they are suggesting items from a service like yours.

They may even be inclined to offer a great testimonial with their experience that can show up on their social media profiles for everyone to see.

Customer Management

Customer management is a very important skill to have when dealing with internet marketing. You will basically be building up a list of emails which will potentially become customers for other projects as well as your current available products.

The email list that you are building is growing with the use of your squeeze page and other opt-in subscribing methods. By making use of these options the email addresses that you are collecting will be worth something later. They are all giving you permission to send them email solicitations later on. This is a very important part of building your email list.

Email List Management

You will want to make sure that your email list only has unique addresses otherwise you will end up sending multiple emails to the same person who really will not help you out very much.

In fact, it may even annoy them a bit if they are receiving a large amount of spam emails from a company like yours. It is a great idea to go through your mailing list then delete any duplicates that have appeared on your mailing list for later.

Newsletters

One of the best ways to ensure that your email list is up to date with all of your products is to send them newsletters.

Newsletters can be comprised of a variety of different pieces of information. The newsletter is a great way to talk about any changes that have been made in the lineup of your products.

Any new additions to your products are a great way to let everyone know that you are expanding what you are selling without leaving anyone out of the loop. Newsletters can also contain reports and articles that are useful to the niche that your products deal with to provide some more information about what is going on in that niche.

Utilizing Autoresponders

If you have an autoresponder set up with your email gathering software you could make it so email addresses that get added to your list automatically start receiving marketing emails as soon as they have joined.

Autoresponders are a special service which can be added to your email campaigns. Each autoresponder is different and will offer different degrees of usability. Choosing an option which offers support and analysis tools is always a great opportunity to ensure that you are reaching your audience correctly.

Accepting Payment Processing Online

Payment processing is a very important topic. It is the way that you will be getting paid with once you sell a product. You cannot simply sell online without having a payment processing option available to you to use.

The most important thing that you need to remember is that payment processing is only available for some programs with some third party services.

Using a service such as PayPal – http://www.paypal.com -is simple to set up and only requires a few security additions to have a fully functioning account.

A merchant account is also possible and requires you to get together with a company that you are eligible for to start accepting payments from buyers.

Using PayPal

PayPal Buttons are one of the simplest options to implement into a website.

They are basically designed however they are needed and can be placed on any website. The service has a built in tool to allow you to create the PayPal buttons to be paid through without having to manually code them.

The tool provides you with a simple interface where you can enter the amount that you wish to receive with the PayPal service and how you want it to look.

Once the process is complete, PayPal produces the button and the code that you simply cut and paste into the HTML of your website or pages that offer products.

This simple method cuts out many of the middle man services and provides prompt payment that is also secure and protected against fraud. This method makes it very simple to accept payments online.

The PayPal service is also one of the best options available for seller protection. Those who have been affected by a reversal of funds can dispute the service and get their money back by a simple process. Various types of goods are covered even digital goods and intangible items.

These items are especially tricky to sell online because the person could state that they never received them or have had errors getting their items.

Of course PayPal allows the service to provide attachments in an effort to stave out inaccurate claims of not receiving items and the like.

Merchant Accounts

Merchant accounts are possible to get started with by finding a merchant account service for payment processing. You will be asked to fill out a form with all of your information that you then must send to the merchant account service. They often allow you to fax in your documents such as the forms, your identification card, a void check and other verification materials so that your account can be created quickly and within a prompt time period.

Once the merchant account is created it needs to be connected to the website to be able to access the merchant services. They will generally offer you a small tutorial on how to complete this portion which is usually manually implemented for each item.

Merchant accounts can also be tricky because they need to be connected to a bank account where money is deposited and withdrawn from. They will generally deposit funds for the sales you generate.

The service will automatically deduct the service fees and membership fee from the account once the payment period comes around. This is where you need to keep money in your bank account otherwise you could risk overdraft fees and the like.

If you do not implement a payment processing service, you will more than likely not be able to receive payments from your sales online.

Some alternatives are through Clickbank with affiliate sales – http://www.clickbank.com -and Google AdSense – http://adsense.google.com -for advertising.

They both will send checks for the amount that you are due after a certain period of time. These checks can then be deposited into a bank account under your name.

So the main reason why you want to have payment processing online available to you is so that you can accept just about any form of payment.

The ability to accept credit cards/ debit cards/ check cards/ e-checks and so many other options far outweighs the small fees if applicable. This makes it possible to be able to accept the payment types that are most commonly used with your service to ensure that you are able to get your money for selling your or another person's products and services.

Digital Product Sales and Delivery

Digital products are one of the most common types of products that you can sell online. These are usually e-books that come from a digital online retailer.

Clickbank

One of the largest repositories for digital products is known as Clickbank. Clickbank is an online digital retailer that offers downloadable products such as software and eBooks.

They make is simple to list, promote and purchase the digital content that is for sale. One of the best things that you can do is take a look at the selection of products that are available through Clickbank to get a feel of what is making great sales.

Clickbank provides several categories which house thousands of digital products. By creating an account with Clickbank you can easily become an affiliate marketer and start selling other people's products. The products come complete with a squeeze page, sales copy, thank you page and much more.

All of these resources come free and only require you to promote them to generate sales. This is done by visiting a product that you would like to promote and finding their affiliate services link.

You will simply place your affiliate ID that is created when you create an account with Clickbank into the box and generate all of your links for the products you wish to promote.

The only thing left to do is promote the affiliate link and make sales. Once you have accumulated sales you just need to wait for payment. That is about as easy as it gets.

 Some affiliate products have very high conversion rates and great bonuses for getting a sale of their product. This will provide a percentage of the sale to go to the promoter as payment for getting the sales.

These can easily be as high as 75% of the purchase price going straight to the promoter. This makes it possible to make a large amount of money if you naturally have the talent to sell other people's products.

The Manual Process for Digital Product Sales and Delivery

Of course not everyone can use options such as Clickbank to generate sales and receive payments. If you fall under this category then it is time to build the autoresponder service that sends out a product once you have been sent the payment for the product.

This is made possible through a service such as PayPal or a merchant account which can be attached to an autoresponder. Once attached, you will be able to seamlessly send products directly after you have received the payment for the service.

Creating an autoresponder for payments

Many autoresponder services are very simple to set up. Many provide step by step services to set up the autoresponder for sales. The process will usually involve connecting the PayPal or merchant account to the autoresponder service and making the right parameters set for payments.

Once a payment is processed through a specific processing step such as paying the amount $XX.XX where "X" represents any number that is set with the service, the autoresponder sends the files which are part of the sale to the email address that is provided by the buyer.

The buyer receives their digital goods and they can enjoy them at their leisure.

Setting up the services with multiple products
Since it is likely that you would be selling multiple products, you would need to follow the above instructions once again for each item that you will be selling with your account.

Once all of the products have been allocated with the service, you will be able to enjoy having multiple products being sold between several accounts with the only additional work that you have to do being to continue to promote the products to generate sales. The manual method can be replicated in several different but requires knowledge of how to work several programs.

Harnessing the Power of HTML Editors

HTML editors are simple to use products which allow you to directly edit HTML (Hyper Text Markup Language).

As a skill, editing HTML is one of the most important things that you can do while being a webmaster. HTML is not so difficult to learn, especially with several of the HTML editors now having graphical user interfaces where you can select all of the attributes for the document without having to manually type them out.

This makes the creation of HTML documents very simple to do and can really increase the abilities of most completely new users of HTML.

Learning the basics of HTML is not a bad idea either. It is always beneficial to have working knowledge of HTML in order to troubleshoot any problems which may occur in any selection of text.

Mostly you will need to know HTML in order to create your own landing pages and make changes to existing pages to give them a customized feel.

By using an HTML editor the process is simplified by allowing access to tools which will make it possible to create websites in a drag and drop sense rather than a manual data input sense.

Making use of FTP

An FTP server (File Transfer Protocol) is designed to make it much easier to move files and website components onto the server for storage and assembly. FTP transfers can be done in three main way:

Using Windows Explorer

Windows can easily connect to an FTP server using any Explorer window. By typing in the address to the FTP server into the location bar in the window, you will open up the FTP service with the folder. To accomplish this you will need to FTP address of your server.

It is usually the same as your domain name with the prefix "ftp://yourdomainname.com" instead of "http://www.yourdomainname.com".

Windows Explorer will open up a field asking for your username, password and whether or not you would like to connect as a guest. When you connect using your hosting username and password you can see the files within the server as if they were a file on your Windows computer.

Making changes to the files located within your server can cause your website to become corrupt and not work anymore. Make changes to the files with caution.

Using a Browser

The browser option is the safest for most users. You will need to navigate the browser to your web host. Login using your username and password and locate the FTP information.

You may be able to log into the FTP server using the browser via the web host. If this is true, then the FTP access will be limited to a file manager type service which you can edit via the web host.

The same process can also be followed for the Explorer
Window in the browser but some browsers cannot handle
the FTP access. Instead a directory listing of all of the files
will be made with all of the files accessible
but not changeable through the browser interface.

Using an FTP Server Software Solution

There are several FTP solutions available that use software
to create secure connections to servers with fewer errors
and risks. They all work in a similar fashion, once installed
they can be accessed from the computer system to load an
FTP server by using the username and password to gain
access to the FTP domain.

Once access is provided it is possible to copy, edit, delete
and create files as well as downloading existing and
uploading new files to the server. The advanced tools of the
server software are very versatile and can make is possible
to really edit websites with much greater ease than other
options.

Three free FTP clients that are available on the web are:
http://filezilla-project.org/
http://www.coreftp.com/

http://www.coffeecup.com/free-ftp/

There are also several paid options available on the market that offer advanced access to FTP servers as needed. These are only recommended for experienced users who understand the inner workings of the file systems on their servers.

It is good to have FTP access skills because it can provide you with several options to edit the website, store files and choose how the website handles the data that is kept server side. Having direct access to the server can also provide possibilities to manually install software that can be used on the website to handle more complex functions of the website.

Graphical Skills

Graphics are an integral part of the internet with websites in modern days. Graphics are what create a vastly different scene on a webpage canvas that was available a decade ago. Graphics can come in a wide variety of different formats and can provide transparency in their layers in order to create dynamic looking websites. Graphical skills can come in 3 different types of skills.

First off it is the photography skill. Photography makes it possible to create realistic graphics using photographs taken from the physical world and applied online.

Photographs can provide a sense of realism on websites where it is not uncommon to see websites with little or no graphics aside from their sleek interface. The photos can add a human element to any website if the website creator is willing to add in the graphics.

Secondly is the photo manipulation and graphical alterations. These are the types of graphics which are made from existing images and repurposed as needed to fit the web. This is a common use of stock images and can be simple yet elegant depending on the skills of the editor of the images. Most of these images are simple to use and feel very generic as most websites that use them do.

The third option is the graphical artist which hones the skill to create the necessary graphics from scratch. These artists are usually the ones that design the website interface or can create graphics as needed using the available graphical software.

The graphical artist can usually also perform the first two skills as well in conjunction to creation graphics from scratch.

The ability to have access to a variety of skills which can be used in the graphical field are very useful for website creation. If you do not have access to a graphics editing program to create graphics you can choose to hire another professional to make the graphics that you need.

A decent graphics artist will be able to create whatever types of graphics that you may need for your website. It is always a great idea to have someone with the proper skills available to produce the services for graphical skills. This is always a better option to use than premade website templates which are often used by several hundreds of websites.

Unit 3: Putting It All Together -Various Online Money Making
Systems

There are all different kinds of money making systems that are available right now which are currently creating a large portion of revenue for those who are taking advantage of the systems.

Imitating these systems will provide similar results and can even surpass the previous results depending on what the niche is that the internet marketer has chosen to take.

It really is a difference between niches as those with a fast paced market may create sales right away while others may take some time before any real sales begin to come in.

Before these money making systems will work for you, you will need to be able to put the system together so that it will work for your specific niche.

You can really compare the online money making systems to a garden. When nourished with all of the proper care, the crops will give several opportunities to collect produce.

If you skip a step in the process or simply neglect it, you will either get a poor return or nothing at all. It really depends on your dedication to the money making system to have the results that you expect to see.

Next Step -choosing what YOU want to do online to increase your
income.

This is where you have your choice of creating your online internet marketing fortune. You need to choose what you will be doing to create your schematic and start earning money in a really responsive way.

You will need to choose what you want to focus your niche on and get out and simply do it. In this following section, we will be providing basic step by step blueprints which you can follow to prepare for creating your own online revenue streams from internet marketing.

These blueprints will be designed for you to improvise and make changes as you see fit to make your online marketing the most profitable for your needs.

Blueprint One: Building Websites Or Blogs to Monetize with

Advertiser Revenue

For this blueprint you will need to have access to a web host, and software to create your website or blog. Fortunately, a variety of web hosts make it possible to create websites and blogs with little to no effort.

Building a Website for Ad Revenue

The creation of a website for advertising purposes is simple to do with any niche. This is the process which you should take before creating a website to ensure that you are getting everything that you need to be able to get your website off the ground.

First you need to select a niche that you will be working within. By researching your niche you could see how popular it is and whether or not you will be able to get traffic to your site by natural searches or not. Once you have decided your niche, you will then need to move onto selecting a domain name to attach to your website for advertising revenue.

The most common option to look into is a domain registrar service which is bundled alongside a hosting company which can provide simple website building tools.

Such services like these are:

Go Daddy http://www.godaddy.com

Host Gator http://www.hostgator.com

Both are very useful in creating simple websites which can host content that is relevant to the niche to generate traffic. These options have generally low cost hosting with minimal cost domain registrar costs.

A simple search online for coupon codes for Go Daddy for instance will provide coupon codes which can reduce the costs of registering a domain by a large percentage and even provide a free one for one year.

Registering a domain name should be done carefully to really maximize its relevance to the niche that it is playing into. The domain name should contain a keyword from within that niche which gets a good amount of traffic.

For advertising revenue, it is a great idea to create a direct keyword phrase in the domain name. For instance, a domain name that incorporates video game rentals would want to use the keywords "video game rentals" in the domain name.

For example - this can be built in the following ways for a domain name:

Videogamerentals

Videogame-rentals

Video-gamerentals

Video-game-rentals

Gamerentals

Game-rentals

These are only some of the combinations which may be available for purchase through a domain name registrar.

In many cases a very popular niche such as video games or video game rentals will be very competitive for these domains and they will more than likely be taken up relatively early.

To make a domain that is more targeted, additional keywords should be added to the domain for more possibilities. These are examples of domain names which will be less likely to be taken within the niche:

Action-video-game-rentals
NewYorkGameRentals
NewestFunGameRentals

Of course there are multiple methods to get shorter domain names which are also more valuable towards making it simpler for your visitors to remember your website URL. These are options to shorten your domain name:

A-Video-Game
AllVideoGames
1FunGameRental
4GameRentals

Although it is a common practice to add numbers to domain names to mimic the domains without the numbers in its stead, it is much better to avoid them whenever possible in an effort to make the domain easier to remember and type in without confusing common words such as "for" instead of "4".

Once a proper domain name has been chosen, it is time to look into a domain name extension. These are commonly ".com", ".net", ".org" and
many others. Other top level domain extensions can range in price from very affordable to expensive in terms of pricing. A ".com" domain extension is the simplest for your website visitors to remember in many cases.

Once a domain has been created, it is time to create the web page using the hosting package that you have chosen. Starting a simple website will generally not require a large amount of hosting so a basic hosting plan will
be easy to choose for a basic website.

If you are using the site building tools available with the hosting service, there are several templates that are available to use. These templates simplify the creation of the website by putting in the base framework for the site.

Once you choose the "frame", you simply need to populate the website with content. The content will need to be a source of articles or other content that is original. The content should employ SEO with keywords that target the niche.

Once the content is created for the website, and the website is live and available to the public, it is time to connect it to an advertising revenue service.

AdSense is a common option for most internet marketers to utilize. AdSense is available through Google which provides complete instructions on setting up the AdSense account with their service. Once the AdSense account is live with the website, you will need to continue to add content to the website where the ads are displayed in order to get more traffic which will eventually increase your revenue received via AdSense.

There are many other ad revenue services that are available. These services are usually designed to pay per a set amount of clicks on the ads or a certain amount based on the ads themselves.

Creating a Blog for Advertising Revenue

Blogs use pretty much the same method as the website creation. You could make use of a hosting service alongside a domain registration service to create a website for a blog. Go Daddy actually offers blogging accounts for an affordable price range. These will come preinstalled with the blogging software of your choice such as Joomla, WordPress, Drupal and others.

Wordpress

http://www.wordpress.org

WordPress is a recommended option because of the simplicity to manage a blog as well as the ability to customize the blog to work as needed.

Choose a domain name which is relevant to your niche. During the setup process you will be asked to name the WordPress blog. It can be changed later if you decide it does not fit well with your blog. Once the setup is complete, you will want to log into the WordPress blog administration account.

You will need to travel to your domain name and find the directory where WordPress was installed. WordPress is typically installed into the root folder of the server. So to log into the WordPress administration panel you would navigate to www.yourdomainname.com/wp-admin and you will see a prompt for your WordPress access information.

During the setup process you had to choose a username and a password for the WordPress account. Enter them here to advance to the administration panel.

The administration panel allows you to post content, change the theme and add plugins to the WordPress installation. The WordPress installation will be very plain at first. You can browse available themes using the theme viewer to choose a professional looking theme or a theme which fits your niche.

You can install the theme directly through the admin panel.

Once this is done, you should start creating content for your website. The content should match your niche and have some SEO practice with keywords and proper formatting. Post the content to the blog using the post options.

The next step is to add in WordPress plugins which make it possible to display advertisements on your site. You can also search for plugins using the plugin search in the WordPress admin panel. Find a plugin for Google

AdSense which allows your advertisements to be placed within posts or on the side bar.

Without a proper plugin, AdSense will not work with WordPress based websites because of some minor code configuration. The plugins help circumvent these limitations and make it possible to place the AdSense ads on your blog site.

Next you will need to follow the process to attach Google AdSense to the blog site. You will need to follow the general process outlined by the Google AdSense service.

Once the website is active with Google AdSense properly configured on the website you will only need to keep adding content to the site and increase the amount of generated traffic using various methods. With the increase in traffic that makes its way to the website, the more of a chance that advertising revenue will be gathered from visitors which interact with the ads.

Remember that other advertising revenue options will also be simple to implement but they will be different to configure and will have their own service advantages and disadvantages. It is not uncommon for a blog to use an option other than Google AdSense.

Blueprint Two: List-Building in Niche Markets – to profit with

affiliate marketing.

Creating a list building websites can be accomplished by choosing a domain that fits the niche market topic. You will need enough time to create a website that has a simple request to get the email address of your visitors. This can be done with nearly any website which can make use of a mailing list or other opt in service which asks for the email of the visitors.

By providing valuable content which can be enjoyed by the visitors, they can be convinced to join a mailing list to be notified about new topics or other information. One of the other methods which is common is offering a free gift in exchange for the email address to solicit emails.

To accomplish creating a list building service which can use scheduled emails and autoresponding services, you can look into a service known as Mail Chimp available at http://www.mailchimp.com with several options.

The Mail Chimp service allows their users to store up to 2,000 subscribers, send up to 12,000 emails per month free of charge. The service works as a forever account with no expiring trials and no contracts. This is especially easy to use because there is no credit card required.

If you need more than these generous amounts of mail list services, there are several great options that are available and affordable for any list building needs.

Using affiliate products as a marketing point to sell to your mailing list is one of the easiest ways to generate funds. To accomplish this you will need to find valuable affiliate products which are offered at a great value.

Once you find a couple of dozen or so, you need to compose email messages to market the products to your mailing list.

The emails should start off with a description of the product which lists the highlights. Write up the emails with calls to action to visit the affiliate site. The affiliate link should have your referral ID included to credit you with any of the sales that are generated through your emails.

Creating well written emails which are designed to sell the products will provide greater chances of selling the products. By using affiliate products that offer higher payouts in your marketing emails, you will be able to earn more with every sale that you generate through these emails.

Once you have created a few emails to send out, you can set them to be sent out with the autoresponder service of Mail Chimp. With scheduled emailing, you can provide your subscribers with well spaced advertisements to affiliate products. Simply add in a few more products every week to have a large set of products to market to subscribers. You will begin to see sales of these products over time. High conversion rates are possible with nicely written email copy.

A few tips to remember about emails:
Email messages should not be too long. Anywhere between a couple of hundred words to about 600 words or so is a great amount to offer more information about the products or services. If the email is too long, the subscriber may get bored and simply skip over the message.

Take a break between trying to sell something to your subscribers and make some valuable emails with information that will keep your subscribers interested in staying subscribed. This is one of the best ways to keep them interested and possibly choose to make a purchase decision in the future with other emails.

Blueprint Three: Developing and Marketing Your Own Products

One of the most rewarding methods of internet marketing is developing and marketing your own products. By doing this, you will be able to produce a product which others can purchase and use.

Creating a product is not always the easiest thing to do but it is always a way to market something within a niche that you may be very good at. Creating a product really depends on the audience and whether or not it will sell.

To do this a little bit of market research is required before you begin working on creating your product. First check the market to see whether or not it exists already.

If so, then you have two options, make your own product and compete or understand the existing product and expand on it as an additional product which could be marketed. If the product does not yet exist, it may be a sign that you are able to make money off of the idea. Make sure before you start that there is indeed a demand for the product you wish to develop and market.

Once your research has been concluded and you can safely proceed with creation of a product which may fair well in the market, you need to then research your product and find out everything that you need to offer with your product in order to make it sell.

Look for similar products on the market and understand how much people will be willing to pay for it. Make sure it is worth your effort to create the product and attempt selling it before you actually take the time to do so. If you are simply interested in selling a new product, one of the best things that you could do is purchase a project from someone else and market it for yourself. This option requires that you have money to invest in such an option though.

You can always think about joint ventures as well. This is a partnership in which you could create a product in conjunction with another creator, designer or other entity and then market it getting your fair shares of the profits.

Blueprint Four: Offering Services To Other Webmasters

There are many reasons why a webmaster would like to take advantage of your services. They are often pressed for time or simply do not have any free time to do many of the functions that they need done with their own websites.

This can be due to a busy schedule or simply not knowing how to do a portion of the work when creating a website. You can offer your services to other webmasters and get paid or your efforts easily.

It is always a great idea to sell your services in areas where you have a stronger understanding of the website creation services. You can simply learn to perform the following services partly or in whole to market your services to other webmasters:

Technical Services

Technical services are always in demand by several companies who simply do not have the time to do it. They will be able to pay you to set up websites, install blogs and do several other tasks which are not always simple to perform.

Since many of these businesses are willing to pay you to do these tasks you can pretty much charge as much as you like for the services. As long as it is not grotesquely high of a charge, most businesses will want to pay your prices for your expertise in performing these functions for them.

The efficiency of the service is often what they are looking for and the faster that you are able to crank out the services the better because they want to move at a fast pace.

The more of these simple technical services that you learn how to perform on websites the better the chances are that you will be able to find work performing the tasks. Keep in mind that not everyone will have some of the abilities that you have to perform some of the simple portions of creating a website. The best thing that you could do is make use of your knowledge in a way that can make you some simple money for your knowledge.

SEO/SEM

Search Engine Optimization and Search Engine Marketing are a great way to make money by providing services for other businesses. By providing SEO services for websites, you can help to optimize the content and increase the possibility of improving the sales of the website.

Search Engine Marketing is also a great method of improving traffic to a website to make it possible for more sales to be possible. This is one of the best options for those who understand the inner workings of search engines to make use of them in a way that could boost the usability of a website.

The ability to perform search engine marketing through various methods is also greatly in demand. Understanding how to properly market via paid search results is always a valuable skill. Instead of businesses and webmasters wasting their time and money creating ads that will not work, they can contract you instead to make their advertisements which will promote them better and receive much more traffic.

Website/Graphic Design

If you are able to create websites or generate graphics, it is always a great opportunity to sell these as a product which can be useful to other businesses. Website designs are always in great demand and the more
professional the design is the more can be charged for the design. It is not uncommon for buyers of designs to want to have the full usage rights to the design. This is to prevent infringement and the ability to copy the design of the website for other site usage.

The same is generally true about graphic design as well. Marketing the ability to create graphics will usually be one of the interesting options to work with.

Designing graphics will really be something that will take some time to work with since clients who need the graphics will often need several revisions of the graphics before the job is done. This can be a lucrative use of a real talent though.

Using premade templates is not always something that website owners will want to do. They want to be able to have fresh websites that are not like others on the web right now. Having a genuine talent of creating designs will always be able to bring you work opportunities.

Make sure that you understand how to work well with many platforms and several types of coding to be able to sell to different types of markets. The best option to take advantage of is always the one that is available when others are unable to provide services for it.

Copywriting

The ability to write good copy – words that sell -is always one of the many qualities that are sought after by companies. They need writers to generate copy for a variety of different products and services. By selling your copy writing abilities you can market it as a product to other businesses. It is a very efficient method of making money.

The strong key points of copy are to sell, sell and sell so this is a quality that you should possess if you wish to market your copy writing services.

The main thing that is important about copy writing is the fact that you will need to be able to write relatively well. Excellent writing skills are always in demand and can land you better work that can pay relatively well.

Content Creation

Content creation is always important for websites. Content is what is used to rank on websites as well as the product which draws the visitors to the website.

Creating content such as articles and other types of media can be a simple way to make some money. Articles and media can be marketed at any given rate. Most of the time, businesses will be trying to get the best deal on this content when they purchase it from the creators.

This makes it possible for the content to be made at a relatively low price to be used as unique content on websites or even in publication print.

Product Creation / Information Products

You can create products for other businesses such as digital products. Another thing that you can create is informational products. Informational products can include everything from videos to resources such as ebooks and reports. These are some of the most versatile products which can be sold on the market.

Other companies are always looking to purchase products which they can rebrand and use to give away or sell and this makes it possible to make money selling these products as a service.

Wrap Up

So there you have a pretty good overview of internet marketing opportunities for Cruisers.

So now what?
the best place to go next is my Web Site:
http://www.moneyforcruising.com
Sign up for the free newsletter, and look for the
 Cruisers Business Blueprint.
The key is to take things one step at a time, plan your work and work your plan. Starting an Internet Business is not a get rich quick scheme. It requires planning and effort, but you can create a full time income that you can control, and a business that will fit into your cruising lifestyle.

to Your Success

Rod Miller

www.ingramcontent.com/pod-product-compliance
Lightning Source LLC
Chambersburg PA
CBHW051731170526
45167CB00002B/890